MW00558772

You Did *What* in the Ditch?

Best Wishes!

Dr. John L. Aldana

You Did *What* in the Ditch?

Folklore of the American Quilter

John L. Oldani, Ph.D.

Reedy Press
PO Box 5131
St. Louis, MO 63139, USA

Library of Congress Control Number: 2011920407

ISBN: 978-1-935806-01-1

Please visit our website at www.reedypress.com.

Design by Jill Halpin

Printed in the United States of America
11 12 13 14 15   5 4 3 2 1

CONTENTS

Acknowledgments   ix

Preface to the Quilt: A Personal History   xi

Chapter 1
What Is Folklore?   3

Chapter 2
Fabric Folk Art   9

Chapter 3
Quilt Vocabulary   15

Chapter 4
The Folk Naming of Quilts   27

Chapter 5
Superstitions: Folk Beliefs and the "Perfect" Quilt   33

Chapter 6
Quilters' Sayings and Proverbs   47

Chapter 7
The Folk Poetry of Quilting   59

Chapter 8
Aunt Jane of Kentucky: The Quilt in Proper Perspective   79

Afterword: The Quilt Reproduces!   91

Research Methodology   95

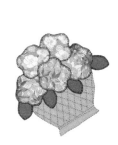

Dedicated to

My wife, Carollee,
who has literally documented our family in quilts, and supported all my
crazy ideas about collecting folklore.

To my kids, Matt Oldani, Susan Oldani Hendrickson, and David Oldani,
who have endured years of my endless discussions about folklore; lived
and practiced, as experiments, the hundreds of various folk beliefs
I tested; schlepped "tons" of quilts to my presentations or exhibits;
and did all with a rare patience! Thank you for what you have become
despite me! I have been blessed!

Acknowledgments

You've heard the expression, "It Takes a Village," right? Well, just about that many people have been a part of my research. As a folklorist, I have been involved with quilts as a participant observer, served as interviewer, judged quilt shows, and have met hundreds of quilters who were very gracious in sharing their lore with me. I am grateful for each and every one of them and, in some cases, their patient and understanding spouses!

But I would be remiss if I did not mention some special people. The late Cuesta Benberry served for years as my primary source. She was a good friend and confidant; the quilting world and I miss her very much. Jesse Reece was the quintessential folk quilter. She managed a pig farm with her husband in Belleville, Illinois, and quilted all her other waking hours producing hundreds of quilts, mostly machine quilted. But her pattern collection was superior and is now in a museum available for researchers. Jesse was a generous person; she is greatly missed. Jean Ameduri, a quilting friend for decades, is tireless in her "quilting connections." She has been active—not a strong enough word—in setting up quilt clubs, quilt shows, international connections to quilting (even travels the world to find it!), and is an exemplary steward with her time, talent, and treasures helping the less fortunate.

I have received encouragement from Hallye Bone, Lois Mueller, Carol Kolafa Ludwig, Jean Ray Laury, Fran Collins, Judie Bellingham, Frank Foley, Barbara Gambrel, Denise Poepsel, Dr. Richard and Aggie Wunderlich, Suellen Meyer, Pat Robinson of the Kuna Indians, the late Leona Rhodes, the Thimble and Thread Quilt Guild in St. Louis, Missouri, and Sally Garoutte's *Uncovering* "gang" over the years. Many,

many more informants cannot be quantified; I hope they understand. They have been influential in ways they do not even recognize: their quilts, their passion, and their historical knowledge. My grandmother, Cecilia Knez, my mother Mary—both missed very much but continued inspirations, and especially, my wife, Carollee Donley Oldani, have been constant in their support but especially in their enthusiastic love of quilts. I hope I represented all of you well in my research. Carpe Diem and Carpe Quiltem!!

PREFACE TO THE QUILT
A PERSONAL HISTORY

Okay, I am not a quilter! I have tried to make memory blocks for my kids' quilts created by my wife for their rites of passage, and I have endured the Dagwood-like comments. But my attempt to get involved in the quilts for my family superseded all the poking fun. My interpretation of what I hoped and dreamed for my kids, through my personally designed quilt blocks, was more important than the workmanship. I know the importance of the quilt in American history, especially women's history. I did not have control of the medium, but my addition to a treasured folk art memory allowed me to appreciate the craft, passion, and dedication of the quilter.

For years I watched my immigrant grandmother make quilts without using patterns, relying solely on her sense of style. She simply cut her fabric from worn clothing—and they had to be pretty worn and not wearable—and preserved the memory of the fabric in an artistic, meaningful, functional, and beautiful piece of folk art. My grandmother had no formal training in design, quilt making, or needlework. She simply "picked it up" without questioning why.

It might be far fetched to conclude that my grandmother, by then a proud American, was following the traditions of the American quilters from the nineteenth and early twentieth centuries. These ladies, who were denied the benefits of society like voting and schooling, were quietly recording a history of their own. In one sense they had no control over the laws of the men in the legislature, so they exercised their control over their piecework. For decades, the American woman quilter produced historical artifacts.

I like to believe that my grandmother had an understanding of that tradition and culture, for she passed on the skill to my mother who eventually surpassed her in talent and artistic design. Did they discuss and understand the quilting tradition they were following? I don't think so. But their quilts were created in the same tradition. They continued to quilt and quilt and quilt for decades.

And I observed.

I earned a PhD in American studies at Saint Louis University. For my doctoral dissertation I chose to do research on the role of the American woman as a facet of the American character. For years I told my students I "worked on women" to get a PhD! At that time, there was a serious neglect of the place of women in American history. There was simply no definitive history and no attempts at remedy. Certainly, I thought, at least recognition of the void could be addressed through preliminary research.

And so I began and observed.

Using primary sources—such as women's journals, letters, diaries, institutional declarations, and interviews housed at Harvard, Vassar, and Smith colleges, among other depositories—I was determined to research the woman's place in American history. At first, I discovered what I had expected: hundreds of documents related to the suffrage movement. This reform has historical validity and has been documented as the major women's issue. Of course, women were not granted the right to vote until the Nineteenth Amendment to the Constitution in 1920, more than one hundred years after the birth of our nation.

Prior to the Nineteenth Amendment, the American woman had been defined as "weak," "feeble-brained," "small-brained," "inferior to men," "inherently domestic," and "must be kept in her sphere for the success of our civilization." Even though Abigail Adams, the wife of our second president, John Adams, had warned: ". . . in the new code of laws, if particular care and attention are not paid to the ladies, we are determined to foment a rebellion and will not hold ourselves bound to obey the laws in which we have no voice or representation," the struggle continued for more than a century.

Yet suffrage was not the only objective. The movement for women's rights in America was filtered through abolitionism, temperance, prison reform, care for the insane, and even fashion. The latter was, perhaps, the most dramatic and concrete symbol of the repressed lives of American women.

For more than fifty years, the corset was an essential element of women's dress. From pre–Civil War until about 1900, the "wasp waist" or the "illusion waist" was considered an ideal for all women as a mark of gentility and femininity. Whalebone provided the means and no method was overlooked in applying such armor. A favorite technique was for a lady to tie her corset strings to a bedpost, expel her breath, and walk as far away from the bed as possible. Sometimes a woman would lie facedown on the floor while another lady, with one foot on her back, would tighten the cords of the stays as tightly as possible. The effects on a women's health were obvious. But corset making became a major industry, and as early as 1866, the demand for corsets was estimated at up to 50,000 per day. By 1900, production of the corset in America was valued at $14 million per year. It is not hard to see why or how reformers for women's rights had a concrete hook in the restricting corset.

Godey's Lady's Book, the most popular publication of the day, had a serious warning for the American woman and her corset-wearing addiction:

> Tight lacing seriously limits, indeed almost annihilates the
> respiratory movement of the diaphragm, for the pinch comes
> on just that portion of the ribs to which this great muscle is
> attached and squeezes them together so as to throw it almost
> or altogether out of work. The lungs do not then appropriate

the proper amount of air; the blood is not completely aerated, and the carbonic acid accumulates. This substance, in sufficient quantities, is, as everyone is aware, a deadly poison, and its effect upon the system when thus continuously present, even though in limited quantities, is extremely injurious.

The editors went on to preach about the "horrible" effects of the corset on the digestive system, the bowels, the liver, and even the nervous system. A full-scale reform, even revolt, was created around the corset. With obvious symbolic ammunition, women suffragettes decried the literal and figurative "keeping the American woman in her place."

Ironically, and simultaneously, *Godey's* was a leader in printing quilt patterns for its readers. The woman who was not in the parade or on the stump protesting the secondary role of the American woman may well have been at home quietly developing her folk art. No doubt, she was aware of the corset reform movement and its connection to women's equality. But she was reforming in another way.

Through corsets, the "devil alcohol," slavery,* reform of prisons, even "hatchetation," and the "Bloomer," woman's place, as secondary to the man, was connected. It seemed that all parts of the American culture, when combined, would succeed in achieving equality for women. But, again, paradoxically, it was the domestic side of the woman, often preached as a reason for inequality, and exemplified in the quilt, which made a significant difference.

While being preached to and exhorted to rebel at quilting bees (many believe Susan B. Anthony gave her first suffrage address at a quilting bee) and other domestic gatherings, the one reform method the American woman kept current was her quilt as a primary document. To her and to many after her, the quilt served as a tangible record of her cultural place. And eventually she was heard!

---

*The role of the American quilt in the Underground Railroad is well documented in the excellent research by Tobin and Dobard, *Hidden in Plain View.*

Interestingly, when the feminist movement was very topical in the late 1960s and 1970s and beyond, and some women were channeling their foremothers in groups like WITCH (Women's International Terrorist Conspiracy from Hell) and SCUM (Society for Cutting Up Men), quilters were unconsciously planting another seed in their own reform. While militant feminist groups were hexing the Stock Market and burning bras, they were also blaming the growing "domestic" art of quilt making for keeping women from achieving completeness. Quilting and such work was, it was argued, not helping women reach true equality. Working on quilts defined second-class citizenship. But quilters, among other "domestic" artists, while continuing to elevate the art of the quilt to incredible standards, did not sit in silence.

In a safe but defiant way, "needlework women" made it clear they chose to preserve history through the art of the quilt. It was a choice screamed loudly and spoken in their true works of art.

Godey's would not recognize the real art that is manifested in the American quilt today. The battle cry is also evident in the current lore documented in this research. Note the pride, the passion, the dedication, and even the defiance connoted in the examples. There is historical precedence here, and it continues to develop with purpose. Quilts are displayed in museums as testimony to an "under-the-radar" historical reform movement, spearheaded by the domesticity of women. There is history in the quilt, and memories, and tradition, but there is much more.

Through her medium of fabric, the American woman remained in control. She may not have had the equality so many were agitating for. She knew it would come eventually. So patiently, she harnessed her honed skills to make a difference. Her fabric, thread, needles, frame, and patterns all belonged to her, and even though they were not headline grabbing, they were used to foment the rebellion. Again, quilting, although mentioned in many primary sources of the time, was not given the significance it really had.

The "lore" of the quilt is as integral as its history. Using the oral tradition, quilt patterns were shared and developed to reflect some meaning. A vocabulary grew within the art. The rites of passage—birth, marriage, and death—serving as the domain of women, were stitched into the quilt. Folk beliefs were initiated and followed and changed and combined in and through the quilt. Legends and superstitions grew up around the quilt both regionally and nationally. Folk customs, social gatherings, even ritual ceremonies evolved. In all this lore, the woman was in control throughout. It was her innovative domain and the quilt her symbol. The folklore of the quilt in America was rooted and continues to grow.

And I have observed and documented.

The lore had to be collected before it was lost forever. As a professor of American studies and folklore at a major university and a visiting professor at several universities, I had an opportunity to collect and preserve this quilters' lore. I established a folklore archive where scholars could research all facets of our lore. A special collection related to the American quilt highlighted the thousands of documents. There was, of course, the folklore of the oral tradition relating to the quilt, which grew exponentially over the years. And there were collections of quilt patterns from as far back as *Godey's Lady's Book* and the *Kansas City Star*, among others, documenting folk naming and history as a corollary.

Eventually, actual quilt blocks of the historically significant patterns were made and catalogued. And as in the *Field of Dreams*, they came! The documented lore of the quilter, already around for decades, was being collected as a function of fieldwork and catalogued. Simultaneously, the art of the quilt was taking on a new life, giving overdue recognition to its place in the history of the American woman.

Simultaneously, my life was taking on a duality: academically and personally. My wife, Carollee, a good seamstress in her own right, started quilting. Again, I am no quilter, but my limited experience threading needles and cutting fabric gave me an appreciation of the meaning of the quilter's lore. Often I was designated as the human pincushion, but I was, again, the participant observer. In a real sense, the traditions of the folk art that is quilting were taking on new meaning, apart from my research.

My wife eventually made quilts for each of our children's graduations and weddings and for the birth of each of our grandchildren. She made charm quilts, scrap quilts, album quilts, more baby quilts, even quilts from the pockets of dusters. There were wall hangings and quilted clothing. And there were more "stashes" and hidden "stashes" and frames and pins on the floor and "frogging" and trips to quilt stores and vacations to fabric stores and clubs and guilds and quilt shows and quilt magazines!

And I observed (not always quietly) and participated.

As my grandmother and mother had done, my wife also created strong messages in her work. Was she doing it consciously following her American sisterhood's tradition? I don't know; probably not. But on reflection, my wife, too, was making her statement. It was her world, her control, her creativity, and most importantly, her legacy. Our family's memories are in her quilts while they warm us figuratively and literally.

And the collection of quilt lore was just like Topsy in *Uncle Tom's Cabin*! It manifested itself proudly, not shyly and quietly, as it had started. The differences are reflected in the folk texts you will read. Passion, pride, history, memory, tradition, equality are all represented with the quilt as the medium. But it should never be forgotten where the lore began, why it started, and what it has always meant. I have observed a dynamic without parallel in any folk group.

I produced quilt shows in the 1970s where two hundred quilts were expected and more than five hundred appeared. They were simply carried in for sharing and bonding, not for showing. The owners had a piece of their family history that HAD to be shared. But more importantly, without bragging, they had something to say about their gender's history. Word spread that it was okay to be a quilter and proud of domestic arts.

I produced thematic quilt shows in various shopping malls around the United States. I directed quilt block contests and had quilts made from the entries. I judged quilt shows around the United States. I was proud to be invited to the first *Uncoverings* research workshop in California.

I observed. I collected more lore of the quilter. I developed a deeper understanding of the "thread" of the folk group, The Quilter.

I present to you my research. I recognize that I am vulnerable to the comments and questions of the quilter who has labored countless hours to present her story and continue the tradition. I do not pretend to be on par with that admirable, and for me unachievable, artistry. It is humbling just to have been privy to my hundreds of informants' lore and their perspective. It has been for me moving and rewarding, funny and absurd, serious and casual, but always germane and reflective of the folk group.

What follows is in no way, and with no intention, a history of American quilting. That has been done very well through the excellent research of pioneers like Ruth Finley and historians like Myron and Patsy Orlofsky, Barbara Brackman, the late Cuesta Benberry, Jacqueline Tobin, Dr. Raymond Dobard, and *Uncoverings*, among many others. They have made it easy for me to learn the basic history.

What I hope I have presented is the folklore of the quilt using "lore" as defined in the accepted field of study. This lore, too, is dynamic and growing; so this work is not exhaustive. I hope that it will create more interest in the need to collect this lore before it is lost forever. I am passionate about preserving the oral traditions of America's folk groups. They can reveal much about our country's history and the character of our citizens.

The early sections of the book are necessary to define what is meant by folklore and how it is studied in academia. There is a science to fieldwork, and knowing a small part of it will enhance the appreciation of what the quilter is trying to do.

Folk art as a "non-verbal" example is introduced to show how the folk, who might be uneducated or not classically trained in any medium, produce valuable and truly artistic work reflective of the culture. I use the Kuna Indians of the San Blas Islands off the coast of Panama who produce blouses, called *molas*, as a perfect example of this folk quality. And the connection to the American quilt will be more evident.

Each chapter describes examples of lore related to quilters as a folk group: speech patterns, vocabulary, naming, folk beliefs, "graffiti," proverbs, poems, and even "down-home" philosophy. The reader, no doubt, will recognize many of the examples I have collected from quilters. It is hard to define a regional approach since quilting has taken on such national significance. But your example of lore may be slightly different from what I have recorded. That makes it even more valuable as a cultural example and valid research text.

Just remember: what is done "in the ditch" stays in the ditch!

You Did *What* in the Ditch?

chapter 1

WHAT IS FOLKLORE?

WHAT IS **?**
FOLKLORE

Remember in grade school when you wrote in your friends' autograph books? Most of them were a variant on the theme of "Remember me." Many of them began: "When you get married . . ." Why did you write them? Remember when you wore something old, new, borrowed, and blue on your wedding day? And then after the ceremony you were pelted with rice? Why did these traditions complete your wedding day? How do you feel when you see a black cat cross your path? Or if you break a mirror? Why do you eat certain foods every New Year's Eve or New Year's Day? Why do you have traditions you never change for Christmas or Easter or birthdays? What happens when you walk under a ladder, put a hat on the bed, or open an umbrella in the house? Do you knock on wood, or step on a crack?

What about your family stories concerning that "special" aunt or uncle that are passed down for generations? Why did you have so many seemingly meaningless verses for jump-rope rhymes? Why do you use the same expressions as your mother? Why do you wear clean underwear when you go out for the evening? Is it really in case you have an accident? Ask your mother. Why don't you play with matches? Did you save a lock of baby hair from your children? Did you throw the bouquet or garter at your wedding?

Why?

All of these things, and hundreds more, are your lore. They represent your dreams, fears, ambitions, philosophies, connections, education, initiations, maturation, and bonding with your "folk." They represent the informal learning process each of us undergoes, encodes, and then applies during all phases of our lives. They keep us grounded, focused, and bonded with our peers. And they are with us all the time! They represent a practicality in this world of unknowns and ambiguities. In essence, they define us.

During your formal education from grade school through college, even, you were taught "formal" constructs like diagramming a sentence or solving an algebraic equation. But have you used these since you left school? Probably not, but often you hear people talk about their rites of passage, like marriage, and what traditions they had to follow. These rites were never taught to you by a teacher; you picked them up just by living.

Were you ever asked if you would mind sitting in Row 13 on a plane? Or stay on the thirteenth floor of a hotel? This is so important that many buildings, including hotels, do NOT have a thirteenth floor! The number is supposed to be bad luck related to the thirteen people at the Last Supper. But no formal educator told you that. You picked it up just by living!

And what about those folk cures or home remedies your mother or father guaranteed to work: potato poultice on burns; baking soda on mosquito bites; whiskey and/or honey in tea for a cold; hot wine to "sweat out a fever"? There was never a formal class in your educational background. Yet these and other cures are still practiced as your grandmother, or mother or father, did. Again, you picked them up by living and you passed them on informally, but importantly.

All this is folklore represented by the oral tradition, the passing on to others, the keeping practices alive, the definition of our folk group. EVERY group has a lore that keeps it together, makes it special, defines its identity, and sometimes even allows for the impermissible! Study after academic study has showcased the lore of children, students, rites of passage in birth, marriage, and death.

There is NOT an occupational group without folklore. The language, rituals, training, even stories around the occupation and its former practitioners creates a fraternity or sorority that keeps traditions alive and produces a "special" bonding.

Folk groups as different and distinct as college students, cowboys, sailors, professors, politicians, salesmen, religious organizations, even pregnant ladies—and many, many more—have lore. As with any generalized lore, the lore of each group reflects its passions, hopes, fears, ethos, or desires.

6

And as a basic rule for collecting lore, it is important to remember that no lore is ever used or applied in a vacuum. The folklorist doing fieldwork among any group identifies patterns and themes that can be used to explain the meanings behind the folk context itself. This can yield definitions of group character traits and even place them in a unique cultural world.

FOLKLORE CRITERIA

Folklore can be all verbal, partly verbal, or even non-verbal. It is important that lore is traditional, that is, follows a standard "formula" for the group. Also, different versions of lore are likely to exist among members of a group, identifying individuals and their region while simultaneously adding to the lore of the folk. The spoken word, as in family expressions or jokes or legends, is the most frequently collected form of lore. Often, however, gestures accompany the text of the lore, like throwing salt over one's left shoulder after spilling some. This, of course, wards off bad luck. No words need be spoken since the gesture is generally known. This is the partly verbal lore, which involves the belief and the gesture attached to it. Then there are the non-verbal examples of lore like the "thumbs up" or "thumbs down" signs or waving with a particular finger (!), also recognized by most people. These require no words!

All are examples of folklore, learned informally, passed down and through groups, often binding and defining a particular one, and applied differently, but traditionally. Simply put, folklore is the common denominator for all of us and defines us as no other context can.

chapter 2

Fabric Folk Art

FABRIC
FOLK ART

Folk art is among the many examples of non-verbal folklore. People, or folk, with no formal training often develop stunning pieces of art with current and classic value. The *molas* of the Kuna Indians who live on the San Blas Islands off the coast of Panama are a stellar example. Their wearable art, a variant of the reverse appliqué technique, is dramatic in its bold, exuberant color schemes, and topical in its depiction of popular culture, local fauna and flora, or their own rituals of living.

The Kuna live in thatched huts and sleep in hammocks without the benefits of "modern" civilization. They have never had formal education of any kind, certainly not training in the world of art and design, yet they produce works of art from mere scraps of material pieced together as cut-outs and highlighted with "nips and pips." Each is an original, with superb needlework, and suggestive of the artistry of the maker without specific identification.

Often the stitches on the mola are so small as to seem invisible and the female mola maker is lauded for her expertise. She then wears it as a blouse—an identifiable folk costume of the Kuna tribe.

Young ladies, having reached puberty, display their first mola, formally announcing their maturation. It, too, is worn as a blouse

and identifies the rite of passage the young girl has undergone. She continues to make molas, and her workmanship, creativity, and artistic sensibility increase with each new mola.

Again, the mola artist is an uneducated woman who produces some of the most highly collectible and expensive folk art in the world. But in the classical definition of an artist, she has not had years of education in the theory of art. What her work expresses is the essence of her tribe—the folk who are bound by their traditions that must be preserved in their fabric creations.

Popular culture, as in their depictions of news they have heard through the oral tradition—a criterion of folklore—is also given a folk representation in the molas. Astronauts, American ships, magazine ads, even Neiman Marcus, among many other American icons, are displayed on their molas. With no patterns to follow, the Kuna woman layers fabrics or adds small pieces of fabric between the layers and then cuts it into a pattern she "eyeballs" and stitches in a reverse form of appliqué.

Often additional embroidery or stuffed shapes are appliquéd to the top of the mola to complete the blouse. Again, no two are alike, but each tells a story interpreted by an uneducated artist. Each mola is a work of art, but as folk art it serves a function as wearable art. Scraps of material are preserved and reused to create beauty and practicality, which is the essence of folk art.

THE AMERICAN QUILT

What the Kuna women did and still do with fabrics in producing wearable art with exquisite detail, American women accomplished with the quilt. In its simplest definition, the quilt is no more than a fabric "sandwich" with batting placed between two pieces of material. A pattern is then stitched into the fabrics, keeping the three parts together. Although this description is the basis of a quilt, it's similar to someone calling the Grand Canyon a hole in the ground!

Arguably, the American quilt is the quintessential example of folk art. Consider the parts: discarded fabric is somehow saved, pieced together in a defined and recognizable pattern, stitched/quilted with another pattern over the fabrics, and then used for warmth. It is and always has been functional and decorative. Often, the pattern of the fabrics tells a story, represents family lore, documents history, or even serves as signs for moral or legal issues.

Through this deceptively simple definition and description, the American quilt, remember, was created and changed by women who were historically regarded as second-class citizens. They were not allowed an education in the formal sense for many decades. Certainly they had no formal education in art theory. They could not even vote until the twentieth century. And throughout all these years of being discounted, the American woman was quietly, conscientiously, and accurately documenting history and her own folklore.

And what her "feeble brain"* has produced! The art of the quilt has evolved into museum pieces, valued at thousands of dollars, creating lore of a folk group that is unparalleled in fieldwork studies. It is functional and practical but beautiful and memorable.

---

*This term was used repeatedly during the nineteenth and early decades of the twentieth century to keep women from enjoying the "rights" of full citizenship such as going to school and voting.

chapter 3

QUILT VOCABULARY

- - - - - - - - - -

QUILT
VOCABULARY

The basis for all examples of folklore, not surprisingly, is the "word" itself. Whether a single word or an expression, one certain folk group—and only one—identifies with the vocabulary as important to their bonding.

There are certainly words used by your family alone, sometimes spoken in front of visitors or strangers who are not part of your group. The word or words are used specifically for the purpose of connecting. For example, everyone has a "thing-a-ma-jig" or a "doohickey" in his or her junk drawer. It could be that catching a cold is the "creeping crud" or the "oogies." And when you eat leftovers, your mother may have said that "musgo" was for dinner—everything in the refrigerator "must go."

Even words for bodily functions or bodily blemishes are part of family lore. School groups, no matter the level, have their own vocabulary as well. This vocabulary is used to connect, educate, compensate, and initiate members. It is the most common form of branding.

Quilters are no different. Their expressions are part of their craft, banter, identification, and bonding, all of which result in the specific "brand" of the quilter. If someone does not know the quilting jargon, she is not part of their "folk." From the earliest forms of quilting in America through present innovative techniques, the quilter has spoken her own folklore.

A complete compendium of the folk vocabulary of quilters is very difficult to collect and document. Each quilter or quilt group speaks a different folk "language." But the basic "dialect" of the quilter does not change. It is a clear identification and a certain bond.

Consider some examples:

"APPLIQUANT" (APPLI-CANT)

Appliqué is a specific form for making a quilt and is often very difficult for a quilter to master. Beginners, often frustrated with the technique, would protest with: "Appliqué! I Appliquant!"

BEARDING

Pieces of the batting get through the fabric and form a **"beard"** on the quilt.

BETWEEN

A short needle; the higher the number, the shorter the needle.

BLIND STITCH

An "invisible" stitch used in appliqué quilting; sometimes used by the Kuna seamstress for her molas.

BUNNY EARS

Formed in two corners when stitching a triangle and square together.

CANDY

A piece of fabric that is half of a "fat quarter."

CC

"I can't quilt, I'm CC!" This quilter argues that she is "color challenged."

CHARMLESS QUILT

Beginners often laughingly refer to their first finished quilt with the self-effacing term "charmless." This is a reference to the revered "Charm Quilt," which has its own lore.

CHEATER

A piece of fabric, sometimes as large as a quilt, baby quilt, or quilt wall hanging where the markings for quilting are already stamped on the material.

CHURCH QUILT

A quilt completed by a quilting group in a church. The meeting, once a week, is a callback to the quilting bee. Often, one of the church members pieces the quilt top together, and when finished the church quilt club puts it on the frame. They sit around the quilt on a weekly basis to complete it. The finished quilt is then used at church events—like annual summer picnics—and won through bingo games or raffles. Many church quilts are embroidered quilt blocks pieced together in traditional settings. Winning such a quilt is a coveted prize to most people, but master quilters often disregard them as "just a church quilt."

COC

"Are you doing it **COC**?"

The quilter is asked whether she is using "Cream on Cream."

CUTTER

A quilt in such bad shape that it can only be used by cutting it up for other projects.

EASE or "EASE ON DOWN"

Making two pieces of different-sized fabric fit together in the same seam. One of the pieces may have to be stretched to make it match.

ECHO

A type of quilting made up of lines of stitches that go around blocks or shapes on the quilt to make the result look like rings that "echo" the shape.

ENGLISH METHOD or PAPER PIECING

Paper templates are used inside the pieces of a block where the quilter turns under the paper.

FART

"Fabric Acquisition Road Trip"—the ultimate experience for a quilter!

FAT QUARTERS

This is not a large coin! Fabric is often sold in smaller amounts—18 × 22 inches—and sometimes referred to as an **FQ**.

FROG

What quilters do when they undo previously completed stitches—rip it, rip it, and rip it! Sometimes they even make it a verb: "had to frog it"; "I'm frogging it."

FUSSYCUT

Cutting a piece of fabric to capture a certain area in the design.

Quilting "IN THE DITCH"

Quilters do not sit in mud and quilt. This term is used for quilt stitches made along a seam line, especially in appliqué quilts.

JELLY ROLL

This is not a fabric pastry! It is a collection of pre-cut fabrics usually measuring 2.5 × 44 inches but can vary in length. The cut fabric is a time saver in cutting and assembling a quilt and often recommended for the beginning quilter to help with color and design.

LAYER CAKE

Using the same concept as a jelly roll where the fabrics are cut for the quilter, the layer cake is usually a 10 × 10-inch square piece of fabric, and each quilt has at least forty squares. The quilt is made from the same line of fabric. Fabric manufacturers are now offering packaged layer cake quilts.

MARKING

Putting a design onto the quilt top prior to quilting in order to provide a guide for the quilt stitches.

NEEDLETURN

A form of appliqué where shapes are traced on fabric, cut out, and then appliquéd and "turned" onto the top of a quilt; sometimes the blind or invisible stitch is used to "describe" the appliqué.

OPP QUILT

A quilt that is raffled off at a quilt show. It is a pleasant "opp"ortunity

OVERCASTING

Stitches used on the edges of the quilt fabric to prevent raveling.

PEANUT

Not the snack, but a piece of fabric that is 11 × 18 inches or even 9 × 22 inches.

PIGS

"Projects in Grocery Bags." Every quilter has many of these that will, they promise, eventually be completed!

PLUMP

A collection of small fabric squares.

"Sarah PUT IN today."

When a quilter was ready to put her quilt top, the batting, and the backing into the quilt frame to begin the quilting process, word got out that she "put in."

PWF

"Pre-Washed Fabric."

QUILTING BEE

This is perhaps the most iconic symbol of the folk art of quilting. American women sat around a quilt frame—and still do!—and they quilted, helping a neighbor or a charity to finish a quilt. Gossip, politics, and sundry news were always exchanged and world issues always solved around a quilt frame.

SHARPS

All-purpose needles.

"How many **SPIs** in the quilt?"

When hand quilting, a mark of excellence was the "Stitches Per Inch" that the quilter used. The smaller and therefore more, stitches per inch were regarded as the mark of an excellent quilter.

STASH

The collection of fabric that quilters own. The stash is more important than anything, including family!

SUMMER QUILT

A quilt without batting, only a top and bottom, technically not a quilt.

"Eventually, word got out that Sarah was on her **THIRD ROLL**."

When the quilt is on the frame and the section open to the quilter is complete, she rolls it up on the frame to expose more of the unquilted area. The number of "rolls" of the quilt depends on the size of the quilt.

TRAVELING

Moving the quilting needle from one point to another through the batting.

WHIP STITCH or "I'M WHIPPING"

Stitches used to seam fabrics on either the right or the wrong side.

WISP

"Work in Slow Progress."

WOF

"Width of Fabric."

WOMBAT

"Waste of Money, Batting, and Time." The sound of the acronym says it all!

WOW

Similar to COC, "White on White" usually refers to fabric.

Depending on the imagination, creativity, or familiarity of the quilter with the terms in the lexicon of the quilting world, folk vocabulary, phrases, or words can be altered and abbreviated. This helps develop the bonding of quilters, and simultaneously confuses the novice. So, the sorority of quilters becomes more special.

Now, you will be able to understand the following statement: "I got some beautiful PWF WOW and then changed to COC and even tried to fuzzycut the last piece and tried some quilting on it and ended up frogging it. My sharps didn't work; it was even hard to ease and square. And you should have seen the bunny ears. Oh, and I even tried doing it in the ditch! This just might become an OPP quilt. All I need now is bearding!"

chapter 4

THE FOLK NAMING

of Quilts

THE FOLK NAMING
OF QUILTS

Where did they come up with that name? Whether it's
a person, object, city, town, village, or geographical or
landscape location, the name has a meaning and a story. It
could be a nickname, used in many different folk groups
for connecting. Or it could be a family name given to a
member for his looks or behavior that sticks with him
for a lifetime. All of these, too, as with all naming, have
a story, perhaps even a legend, associated with them.
Discovering origins is often difficult for researchers since
many names are used in different contexts. But no matter
how the name is used, its meaning, although different in
each case, serves as the glue for many folk groups.

No folk group has a more fascinating or enormous collection of
"names" than quilters. They are ideal representations of the definition
of folklore. They exist in different versions for the same piecing. The
"Wandering Foot" quilt pattern in one region, for one quilter, for example, might be "Turkey Tracks" for another. They are the same pattern
but reflect perhaps a whim or a local fowl phenomenon.

Some names are traditional, another criteria for folklore, and follow
a pattern for decades, as in variations of "Log Cabin." Also, they are
anonymous. The quilter who gave a name to a quilt pattern is rarely
known, but the pattern becomes migratory through oral tradition
and could even have a name change depending on the whim of the
craftspeople and their experiences.

Very importantly, also, quilt names often reflect the history of the time in which they were applied. Women who could not take part in politics, for instance, got involved in documenting history through the quilt. "Whig Rose," "Burgoyne Surrender," "Abe Lincoln's Log Cabin," "Martha Washington's Star," "Dolly Madison's Star," and "Washington Rose" reflect history. Moving westward in covered wagons or on foot gave way to "Prairie Flower," "Road to California," "Rocky Road to Kansas," "Oregon Trail," "Path in the Wilderness," "Wild Geese," "Pine Tree," "California Rose," "Ohio Star," and even "Delectable Mountains," with the dual reference to geography and Jonathan Swift's work. "Prairie Queen" came from the move westward, and legend has it that Calamity Jane went by the same name for a time. Perhaps there's a dual naming purpose here.

The Bible, not surprisingly, has been a source for many quilt names. The "Rose of Sharon" may be the most popular and oldest pattern with Biblical connections and it was often considered the mark of an excellent quilter to make one in this pattern. This is akin to "spiritual perfection" and recognition of a savior. There is "Jacob's Ladder," "Job's Tears," "Crown of Thorns," "Crosses and Losses," "Cross and Crown," "King Solomon's Temple," "Job's Troubles," "Joseph's Coat," "The Rugged Cross," "Road to Jerusalem," and "Tree of Life." These quilt patterns, among many others, underscore more than a quilt design. They speak to a strong religious tradition in American culture. Using the medium of a quilt can preserve and pass on the spiritual culture. Even the "Lone Star" quilt and pattern is often named "Star of Bethlehem."

Quilt patterns celebrate American cities: "Annapolis," "Indianapolis," "St. Louis," "Chicago," "Sacramento," "Kansas City," "Santa Fe," "Phoenix," "Atlanta," "Salt Lake City," "Jefferson City," "Allentown," "Charleston," and "Savannah" are just a few. And states have not been slighted. Every state in the United States has a quilt pattern with folk derivations related to the admission of the state to the Union, some topographical or geologic uniqueness to the landscape, or an historical landmark in the state. But folk whimsy enters into this naming as the pioneer spirit of settling a state is memorialized in quilt patterns. These are represented in the "Road To" quilt patterns: "Road to California, or Kansas, or Arkansas, or Oklahoma" are some of the popular ones. Sometimes the roads are "Rocky," and sometimes they lead to "Heaven," as a synonym for the destination, or to "Fortune," reflecting the gold mines or a better life in another location. But each is different in its piecing, reflecting the folk criterion of different versions of the same text.

Proverbs, folk tales, legends, folk games, and other folklore genres are remembered in quilt patterns: "Robbing Peter to Pay Paul," "Cupid's Arrow," "Friday the Thirteenth," "The House that Jack Built," "Puss in the Corner," "Pandora's Box," "Jack-o-Lantern," "The Flying

Dutchman," "Follow the Leader," "Fox and Geese," "The Chinese Puzzle," "Barbara Fritchie," and even "Carrie Nation." They become a part of what is known as "metafolklore." The story, saying, or tale is well known but is then documented in the tangible and permanent fabric as different from the oral tradition. The pattern itself is then copied and passed through generations of quilters in the folk group.

The pattern "Log Cabin," long considered the "true" American quilt pattern, follows the folklore criteria well, along with demonstrating the creativity of the quilter. Placing the strips of material in different arrangements uses the basic "Log Cabin" theme but becomes "Barn Raising," "Sunshine and Shadow," "Straight Furrow," "Pineapple," among many others. It's the same basic name for the pattern, but the effect is always different and original.

Often quilt patterns were so popular they were "required" to be made as part of any quilter's craft. Some have even given way to stories or folk beliefs because of their consistent popularity. "Lone Star," "Dresden Plate," "Double Wedding Ring," "Irish Chain," "Mariner's Compass," "Bear's Paw," or "Grandma's Flower Garden," sometimes by other names, are considered staples for the dedicated quilter to make. And they give way to more lore. Did "Double Wedding Ring" come from a suitor too poor to buy an engagement or wedding ring? Did "Dresden Plate" reflect the German city and its pottery making? Was the "Lone Star" quilt used as a funeral quilt to be placed over the corpse before the casket was closed? Did the "Irish Chain" reflect the craft from Irish seamstresses? Was the "Bear's Paw" pattern on quilts really used in the Underground Railroad as a marker for safe passage?

Then there is the beautiful, elaborate Baltimore quilt, appliquéd with floral, patriotic, animal, or other motifs. Did it originate in Baltimore? Was it influenced by the German quilting art? Album quilt, friendship quilt, memory quilt, and other generic names used different patterns to inscribe names or dates. But the significance came in the remembrances from the finished quilt and an actual historical document for the ages.

The history of quilt pattern names is a fascinating and elusive study. Because of the oral tradition, where patterns were passed from family to family—or quilter to quilter—it is hard to codify all with certainty. And that is where the discipline of folklore can make a difference. The actual origin of a quilt name is important, but not critical. The use of the pattern, the rationale behind its choice, and the reflection of the culture make it important and charmingly relevant.

There is a great deal of excellent research by quilt historians on the origins of quilts and quilt names. Some have discovered documentation that suggests American quilt patterns have ancestors as far removed as ancient Rome, Greece, or even Egypt. Many popular American quilt patterns, some contend, were possibly British in origin. Preserved quilts, when examined, are often so close in design to those declared as "pure American" that the study of origins of the quilt and its naming is difficult to declare with any certainty. This fascinating investigation, however, lends itself well to the lore of the quilt as folk art.

The names that have been used over the years to describe quilt patterns reflect the folk naming of the quilter. Experiences, memories, religion, history, freedom, philosophies, births, deaths, marriages—whatever the intent of the quilter, the name given to the finished work is the correct one! We have only to be grateful for the migratory nature of the tales that followed and the unparalleled creativity of the artist. "Jacob's Ladder," for instance, becomes important not only for its Biblical reference, but also for its practicality for those seeking freedom in the Underground Railroad. Fabric was pieced, inspired by an intuitive spirituality. The quilt was completed. It was placed on a tree or a fence. When noticed by those escaping slavery, it led the way to freedom—a ladder to freedom and to a haven and a heaven. The folk tale comes full circle. To paraphrase Juliet: by any other name, it would still be a history in fabric.

chapter 5

SUPERSTITIONS

FOLK BELIEFS AND THE "PERFECT" QUILT

Everyone! IS SUPERSTITIOUS

Our belief system, although it may not be connected to an action, is part of our informal learning process.

Black cats, broken mirrors, the number 13, umbrellas opening in homes, hats on beds, catching a bride's bouquet, walking under a ladder, putting shoes on a table—we recognize all of them as causes for something "which could be bad luck for the person who acted." No teacher in an educational system ever taught us these things. We picked them up by living. This is folklore reflecting our fears or even our future.

We may not practice or believe what the omen represents, but we are aware of it, and we subconsciously apply it. The thinking is often simple: What harm would it do? We can't control the future in our rites of passage so we recognize the "object" and just don't dwell on it. Or just knock on wood!

The word *superstition* comes from the Latin "*superstitio*," which means "standing in fear of the deity." As the ancients believed, the gods controlled us in ways we could not know, so what harm is there in recognizing the existence of superstitions? Almost all of our rites of passage—journeys in our lives with significant changes or possible different outcomes—are accompanied with these folk beliefs. Whether we believe that a pregnant woman should be given the food

she craves, immediately; or the bride should wear something old, new, borrowed, or blue; or mirrors should be covered in a home when someone dies, we are recognizing changes in our lives that need to portend good luck. We need some control over the unknown. "Standing in fear of the deity," we try some contagious "magic."

Making a first quilt, or any quilt, connected as it is to the folk traditions of the craft, is similar to a rite of passage. The end product might be functional, but the process is much more involved. Preserving fabric from the waste dump, creating a quilt top with a defined pattern often from scraps, documenting a momentous personal or family happening, or even recording history, the quilt remains a major undertaking that represents pure folk art.

Given the place of quilts in folklore and the bonding of the quilters as a folk group, it is not surprising that folk beliefs (or superstitions) would be important to the successful outcome of the quilt. Here are some beliefs associated with quilting that have been passed on in the manner of the oral tradition, collected from many quilters who continue to "guide" their creativity whether acknowledged or not. Consider some examples.

Love, Courtship, Marriage

✳ When sleeping under a new quilt, name each of the four corners for a man you know and you will marry one of them.

✳ When making a quilt for a man as a gift, always place a feather inside the batting. It will guarantee that he will be forever faithful.

✳ In a quilting pattern, always have a design of a crane, no matter how small. It will ensure a faithful husband. Some lore believes cranes bring babies. Also, a replica of a crane often sits atop a chimney ready to drop the baby in a home.

✳ Young lady quilters should make a "Charm" quilt as their first one to ensure good luck, good fortune, and a happy marriage. The goal is to collect 999 pieces from friends and never to buy any of the fabric. The one thousandth piece should be delivered or discovered "accidentally" pinned to the pocket of her future husband's shirt.

✳ If you start a quilt and never finish it, you will never marry your true love.

✳ Bring a wedding quilt made for the bride and groom to the ceremony after placing straight pins in it. Give each of the guests one of the pins. The "steel" from the pins will give strength to the couple and the energy will be transferred from and to the guests.

✳ In order to have good luck or to find a husband if you are unmarried, on New Year's Eve, take a new quilt—one that has never been used—and shake it out the front door. This gets rid of all the bad luck of the last year.

✳ If the quilting pattern is broken in any way, the owner of the quilt will have a bad marriage.

* If four unmarried girls hold a new quilt at each of the corners and put a cat in the middle of a quilt, then shake it, the corner where the cat leaves the quilt will be the first girl married. Often it is believed she will be married within the year.

* If a quilter is not married and desires to be married, she should never put the final stitch in the quilt.

* No matter how small, the quilting pattern of a quilt must have a heart shape in it to guarantee true love, always, for the owner.

* Before giving a bride her wedding quilt, pin bay leaves to each of the corners and one in the middle of the quilt to ensure true love forever.

* A handkerchief placed into the batting of the quilt will ensure domestic bliss for every owner of the quilt.

* A small glove placed with the batting of a quilt will ensure that the owner of the quilt will have a true and lasting romance. (On Valentine's Day, gloves, signifying true love, were given as a gift from a suitor to his lady friend.)

* If you drop the scissors you use while quilting, it's a sign someone close to you has been unfaithful.

* It is also believed that a wedding quilt must never be made in the pattern of "Wandering Foot" or "Turkey Tracks," as it will cause the husband to "stray" from the marriage bed.

* If you place a feather from a swan into the batting of a quilt, you will ensure that the people who sleep under the quilt will always be faithful.

* If you do not use a quilt pattern of a vine on the border of a bride's quilt, the marriage will be rocky.

* Before getting married, it was believed that a young lady must have thirteen quilts in her hope chest. The thirteenth quilt would be her wedding quilt. Some believed that is why some young ladies never got married!

* Then there is the poem which gives a different version of quilts connected to marriage.

> *At your quilting, maids don't dally,*
> *A maid who is quiltless at twenty-one*
> *Never shall greet her bridal sun!*

(Apparently, this poem was stitched on a quilt from the nineteenth century. One interpretation can be made to the importance of marriage for a lady.)

Luck, Good or Bad

✳ If you sit on a pair of quilting scissors while working on a quilt, you will soon cut a friendship short and bad luck will follow the owner of the quilt.

✳ If a quilting needle or straight pin used during quilting happens to bend, throw it away immediately or it will bring bad luck to the quilter or quilters working on the quilt. Similarly, if you see a bent needle or pin near the quilt on the floor, do not pick it up—more bad luck.

✳ It is good luck to sneeze on a quilt while quilting it on the frame. (This may be related to the response spoken to the person who sneezes: "God Bless You." It is an example of the magic of transference.)

✳ Every quilt should have a piece of silk somewhere on it or in the batting. Silk is the "luckiest" fabric, and the luck from the material will be a "magic of contagion" for the quilt owner.

✳ Around a quilt frame, two people should never be allowed to quilt on the same block; it will bring bad luck to one of them.

✳ Before giving a quilter a needle from a pack, prick her finger to protect her from bad luck.

✳ After making a quilt for someone for a special occasion, the quilter should sleep under it herself for one night to ensure good luck for the recipient.

✳ If you break a thread while quilting, whoever sleeps under the finished quilt will have bad luck.

* Of the thousands of pieces of fabric in a charm quilt, it is believed that at least two of them must be alike and that those who sleep under it the first time must find the identical pieces before they fall asleep or they will have bad luck in the near future.

* In the stitched quilt pattern itself, use a spider web for guaranteed good luck.

* Never give a pair of quilting scissors to anyone. They must buy their own to avoid bad luck.

* If the markings on the quilt for the pattern are not removed before the quilt is given to a person to use, the recipient will have bad luck.

* Never wash a quilt before it is used; you will wash all the good luck out of it.

* Never start a quilt in the form of a star, like "Lone Star," if someone in the family is sick. That person will die before the quilt is finished.

* Never work on a baby quilt while sitting on a bed, and never cut material for a baby quilt on a bed. It will scar the baby for life.

Folk Medicine

* Tie quilting thread around a wart to get rid of it.

* Rub a piece of the fabric used in the quilt over a wart or a boil and say: "Fabric, fabric, do your duty. Make this quilt and me a beauty."

* When someone is ill, make him or her sleep under a new quilt. The love that made the quilt will transfer a healing power to him or her.

Pregnancy and Birth

* When making a baby quilt, never show it to the mother of the baby until the baby is born. It will bring bad luck to the mother or baby.

* Some people believe that if you break a needle while quilting the next baby will be yours.

* If someone wraps you in a new baby quilt before it is used for the baby bed, you will be pregnant during the next year.

RELIGION AND SPIRITUALITY

* If you prick your finger while quilting and get a spot of blood on the quilt, use the water from an Easter service to clean the quilt. Not only does it work perfectly, but also it adds a blessing to the owner of the quilt.

* If possible, have your first quilt buried with you so that your "spirit" sewn into the quilt will not wander searching for a home after your death.

* Never quilt on a Sunday. Every stitch you put in on a Sunday will have to be taken out with your nose. Some say, if you use a thimble, you can quilt on Sundays, because the thimble will keep you from harm.

* Never, ever quilt on Ascension Thursday. It is such a day of reverence that one must celebrate and do no work.

* Never begin a quilt on a Friday. You will never live to see it complete. (This is apparently connected to the death of

Christ on the cross on a Friday; with Friday being the hangman's day; and with Scandinavian lore where Freya, the goddess of broken love, who some say gave her name to love, rode in a carriage driven and pulled by cats. And what follows, of course, is the belief in the specific day: Quilting on Good Friday will bring bad luck to the quilter and to the eventual owner of the quilt.)

✳ Humility Block: It is believed that every quilt should have one mistake in it. Only God is perfect and even the most beautiful quilt has to have one mistake, no matter how small, as recognition of the power of the Almighty. (This belief is debated by scholars. Some question its authenticity. As folklore, it is still being practiced and believed by many quilters, so the doubting is a moot point. However, there is ample evidence in history that crafters believed that their product should have some flaw in it for the same reasons quilters believe. For example, the famous centuries-old tapestry in the ancient ruins of the Rock of Cashel with St. Patrick's Cross in Ireland has many flaws in it. The Flemish artists strongly believed that only God could make something perfect.)

✳ Placing small amounts of salt in the batting of a quilt will ward off evil spirits from those who slept under the quilt. (Many cultures believe that salt has magical powers to drive away evil.)

✳ Hold a piece of the quilting thread in your mouth, or suck on a piece of the quilting thread you are using. The spittle or "spirit" from the quilter will serve to protect the owner of the quilt.

SOCIAL

✳ If you find a quilting needle on the floor, pin it to the left shoulder of your clothing and make a wish. It will come true. (This is analogous to throwing salt over your left shoulder when you spill it. The Latin word for "left" is *sinister*. Placing the needle into the left side of your clothing creates a "contagious magic" that will do away with the demons.)

✳ If you drop a quilting needle and it sticks in the floor you will have company—people you have not seen in a long time.

✳ If you stick a quilting needle or straight pin into your clothing for convenience and it appears just about to fall out, someone is talking about you and not in a good way!

✳ When sharing quilt fabric with someone, always place a quilting needle in the middle of it so as not to harm the friendship.

✳ A quilter should always place a lock of her hair in the batting of a quilt. This will ensure that she will be connected to the owner of the quilt forever.

✳ Never put human figures on a quilt or a picture of someone because the person depicted will visit you at night and could do you harm.

✳ Designing a piece of food from fabric for your quilt, or stitching some design of a food product on your quilt, will guarantee that you will never, ever go hungry.

✳ As you are "frogging," or ripping out mistakes, keep repeating the name of someone as a mantra. This serves as a hex on that person and a therapy to the quilter.

Illinois Quilt

The twelve blocks in this quilt were the winners of the "Illinois Quilt Contest" to design a block that represented Illinois. There were 464 entries, and "Illinois corn" was chosen as the winner. Folk naming, folk tales, folk beliefs, and folk icons, creatively assigned to Illinois, are all represented. The traditions were passed on!

Fan Quilt

Made at the end of the nineteenth century, this quilt is an excellent example of style, piecing, and artistry. The effect is of a fan, but some scholars find the bunting used in an American celebration more descriptive. Either way, the "feeble-minded" artist made a statement!

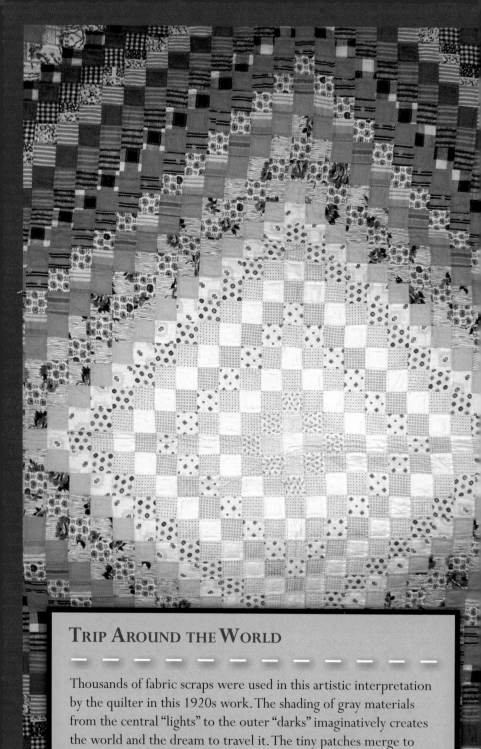

TRIP AROUND THE WORLD

– – – – – – – – – – – –

Thousands of fabric scraps were used in this artistic interpretation
by the quilter in this 1920s work. The shading of gray materials
from the central "lights" to the outer "darks" imaginatively creates
the world and the dream to travel it. The tiny patches merge to
create a flow that is different from every angle.

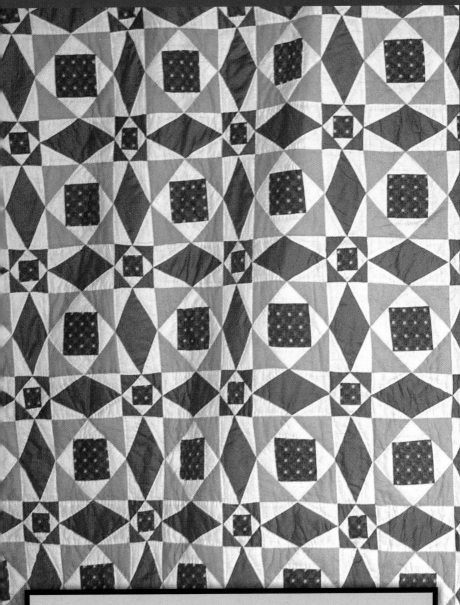

STORM AT SEA

More than 4,000 pieces of fabric were used in this quilt to develop
a variant of this popular pattern. The setting together of the
various shades of blue effectively simulates a storm. The whimsy of
this quilt is that it was made to be placed on a waterbed! The name
of the quilt and its use become interactive!

Stars

An excellent example of a scrap quilt by a quilter made in the 1920s. The patchwork pieces were part of another original purpose—perhaps a dress—but their use in this quilt keep the memory of their histories alive. The quilting adds the creative dimension of the artist.

Hex Signs

A perfect marriage of the art of quilting, folk beliefs, and traditions from the lore of the Amish. Each block in this quilt represent a hex sign, often seen on barns throughout Amish communities. Whether the hope for good crops, a blessed marriage, fertility, or health, each sign served as a reminder of the place of lore in a family's life.

Geraniums

As a perfect example of conserving, creating, and recycling, this quilt was made from the pockets of a lady's duster. They were discovered at a garage sale thrown among scraps of material. The actual quilting around the flowers is done in very tiny stitches, stippling, giving the "discarded" scrap pockets an added dignity. Again, function and beauty, defined in quilts, is well displayed.

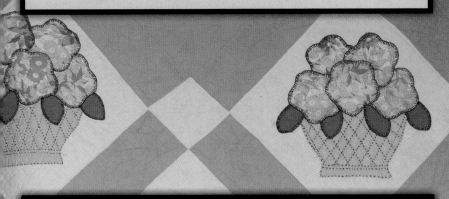

Flower Pots

Done in the 1930s by an immigrant to America, who had never quilted, this quilt not only shows the appeal of quilting, but also the beauty in the creative process of an uneducated folk artist.

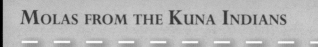

Molas from the Kuna Indians

The Crucifixion, Deep-Sea Divers, Geometric Snake, and the Big Fish are excellent and varied examples of the superior stitchery of the Kuna

woman. Note the many colors in each of them all layered to create an original mola. The stitching keeping the molas together is next to invisible. Deep-sea divers are not part of their culture, but they "imagined" them. Kuna women can relate to the snake, the fish, and the meaning of the Crucifixion, but the personal, stylized examples give new meaning to each one.

PINE TREES

A modern example of the use of color by a quilter. Shades of green in the various trees, from selected fabrics, emphasize the importance of the sense of color identifying an American icon.

JEFFERSON STAR

Known by other names, this quilt from the late nineteenth century is an example of superior workmanship by a quilter who had no formal education but a creative urge to preserve history. The artist went so far as to use dyed blue thread in some sections of the quilt.

* Putting a coin into the batting of a quilt will ensure that the owner will never be broke.

* If you prick your finger while quilting and get blood on the quilt, the first person to sleep under the quilt will get sick.

* If you get a knot in your quilting thread, someone is talking about you. The more knots the worse the conversation about you.

* If you make a quilt for a son to celebrate an occasion, never use the pattern "Turkey Tracks" or "Wandering Foot" or "Wandering Star." It will make him a wanderer the rest of his life and he will never return home, nor will he keep a job.

* Whatever you dream while sleeping under a new quilt for the first time will come true.

* Always put the color yellow in the quilt—no matter how small the piece—as it symbolizes the power of the sun, which will give good health to the owner.

These folk beliefs about quilting underscore the importance of the work, pride, significance, and passion that are involved in the making of a quilt. In a real sense, it is a rite of passage. Not only is the finished quilt a strong sense of accomplishment, but also it is an initiation into a group filled with a sense of history, memory, creativity, and perseverance.

Certainly all of the "faith in the magical practices" to effect a contribution to folk art are not practiced by all quilters. But every quilter can identify with the intent of the belief. Call it a superstition, with some negative connotations, or call it a practice, which can serve as a positive intervention to a prideful undertaking. There is no harm, it is believed, in following such quilting rituals. Most are connected to the usually defined rites of passage: birth, marriage, death. All have the element of the "unknown" in them. There is no certain way to predict the outcome or the timing of each. So why not try to control a result with some whimsy or "proven" practice. What can it hurt?

In psychological terms, all these quilting practices, and numerous others related to daily activities, are called *memes*. Information gets passed around a culture, sometimes for generations. It can be attitudes, beliefs, rituals, customs, facts, myths, and philosophies—whatever—and is replicated. These are successful memes. And the folk group continues the practice.

Whether the beliefs are "truths" or not is irrelevant. The critical aspect is: can the beliefs be passed around and replicated? Quilters—filled with creativity, sensibilities, and purpose—want their inspiration and work to be treasured. They would answer a resounding YES!

chapter 6

Quilters'

- - - - - - - - - - - - - - - - - -

Sayings and Proverbs

QUILTERS'
SAYINGS AND PROVERBS

Want to express yourself? Write it on the walls. It
started with the cavemen. Leave your message behind
where someone can read it. Thoughts about your
culture? Scrawl it on the wall. Essentially, "graffiti"
in its various forms has always been part of human
culture. Its spectrum and meanings are wide, but the
purpose is usually the same: getting attention!

Scholars have debated the importance of all the anonymous
sayings, art, symbols, and labels for decades. Universities even
offer classes in graffiti. The premise is that folk groups feel a need
to be heard, understood, and united. The spoken word may be said
to deaf ears, but what is written—from an anonymous source in
a public place—can and will be remembered. And the medium
becomes the message.

Bathroom walls, bumper stickers, T-shirts, tote bags, buttons, and
pins are all modern-day cave walls. Any expression or opinion
from a folk group can be spoken, worn, or displayed so the
whole world will know its purpose. Instant identification, instant
bonding, instant recruitment, instant spotlight—all this can come
from anonymous "scrawls."

Quilters are a prime example of the modern-day "cavemen." In
fact, they are arguably the BEST example in their passion for
their craft and its monumental tradition. Quilters know the

importance of quilting as a folk art in American history, the art's purposefulness, and its links to the past, present, and future. The vast majority of quilters are women—this cannot be overstated. Quilting allows women to define their importance in a culture where they have been historically discounted for decades. They were the original "green-is-good" Americans in their conserving fabrics and making their quilts not only functional but also beautiful. Women shout it out to the world in their artifacts on which they cleverly scrawl their pride. Recent examples of graffiti underscore what has been stated earlier. Quilters are proclaiming loudly: "We are *choosing* to speak with our needlework and making our statements artistically."

Consider some of the following statements. You will note variations of popular expressions, current topics, "women's domain redefined," self-effacement, a delightful wickedness in the humor, and a clear, funny, but serious caveat: I am a quilter; make no mistake about it. I am very proud of my "job!"

Quilters' Graffiti

✴ A fat quarter is not a body part.

✴ Asking a quilter to mend is like asking Picasso to paint your garage.

✴ Dull women have immaculate homes.

✴ I love quilting and have plenty of material witnesses.

✴ I got a sewing machine for my husband. Good trade, huh?

✴ Before Prozac, there was quilting.

✴ See Sally.
See Sally quilt.
Quilt Sally quilt.

✴ I only quilt on days ending in a "Y."

✴ If I stitch fast enough does it count as aerobic exercise?

✴ Lost: Husband, dog, and sewing machine.
Reward for sewing machine.

✴ I sent my kid to college so I could store fabric in her room.

✴ If there are no Quilting Bees in Heaven, I'm not going!

✴ FABRICOLOGIST RESEARCH CENTER
(More impressive than "my stash" . . . huh?)

✴ I've spent most of life making quilts. The rest I've just wasted.

✴ Make quilts not war.

✴ Working on my PhD: Project Half Done!

✴ My husband lets me buy all the fabric I can hide.

✴ Quilting is the cheapest therapy.

* Quilt. Eat. Sleep. Repeat.

* Quilter's diet: low carbs; lots of fabric.

* Cooking and cleaning are for people who haven't discovered quilting.

* Beware: I have size 12 betweens and I know how to use them.

* My husband is a human pincushion.

* Name Tag: My name is Judy and I'm a quiltaholic. Hi Judy!

* My soul is fed with needle and thread; my body with chocolate.

* My husband said if I buy any more fabric, he'll leave me— I'll miss him.

* I am NOT fabric obsessed; I still have room in my closet!

* Beware: Serial Quilter

* Fabric Slut!

* There is no crying in quilting!

* My sewing machine is smarter than your honor student.

* To quilt or not to quilt? DUH!

* Urban Amish!

* People who are organized are just too lazy to get up and look for it.

* Procrastinate. It frees up time to quilt!

* Because I'm the quilter, that's why.

* Runs with rotary cutter.

* Quilters don't cut corners.

* Don't ever quilt and drive!

* Quilting fills my days, not to mention the living room, bedroom, and closets.

* Beware: All quilters come with strings attached!

* I keep my tables covered with quilting so I won't have to dust them.

* Plays well with others, except a fabric salesperson.

* Sewing forever, housework whenever!

* Do not make me use my quilter's voice.

* Got fabric?

* She who dies with the most fabric wins!

* STASH MANAGEMENT FLUNKIE!

* Touch my scissors and die!

* Quilters hang out on the "seamy" side of town.

* CARPE QUILTEM!

* Warning: This vehicle stops at all fabric shops.

* Quilting: It is what it is!

* When I learned how to quilt, I forgot how to cook.

* Plays well with fabric.

* Think of it as a power tool with thread.

* Robert's Rules: Complicating Quilt Club meetings since 1875

* Will work for FABRIC!

* Show me the fabric and no one gets hurt.

* You know you are drinking too much coffee when you can thread a sewing machine while it's running!

* All quilters lead pieceful lives.

* The "machine quilter" is not really equal to the "real" quilter, but she is close!

THE QUILT HIERARCHY

THE QUILT FABRIC SALESPERSON

Leaps tall buildings in a single bound
Is more powerful than a locomotive
Is faster than a speeding bullet
Walks on water
Gives policy to God

THE MACHINE QUILTER

Leaps short buildings in a single bound
Is more powerful than a switch engine
Just as fast as a speeding bullet
Walks on water if sea is calm
Talks to God

THE MAN QUILTER

Leaps short buildings with a running start and favorable winds
Is almost as powerful as a switch engine
Is faster than a speeding BB
Walks on water in an indoor swimming pool
Talks with God if special request is approved

THE HUSBAND OF A QUILTER

Makes high marks on wall when trying to leap buildings
Loses tug-of-war with locomotive
Can fire a speeding bullet
Swims well
Is occasionally addressed by God

THE QUILT GUILD PRESIDENT

Runs into buildings
Recognizes locomotive two out of three times
Is not issued live ammunition
Can stay afloat in a life jacket
Talks to walls

THE NOVICE QUILTER

Falls over doorstep when entering building
Says, "Look at the choo-choo"
Wets herself with water pistol
Plays in mud puddles
Mumbles to herself

THE "PRO" QUILTER

Lifts buildings and walks under them
Kicks locomotives off the tracks
Catches speeding bullets with her teeth and eats them
Freezes water with a glance and skates on it
She is God!

PROVERBS

A proverb is a simple sentence, sometimes in a metaphor, which captures a whole essay or moral lesson and is an integral part of our folklore. Benjamin Franklin was an expert in his "proverbial wisdom" and created in others the need to educate in a deceptively simple sentence. "Early to bed and early to rise makes a man healthy, wealthy, and wise." Or, "A penny saved is a penny earned." Or, "He who hesitates is lost." Or, "The pen is mightier than the sword." Each of these has a connotation that could be developed into a paragraph but its genius is in its simplicity.

Quilters, too, creative artists as they are, have developed a whole lore of proverbial expressions. Some are derivatives of well-known sayings, and they follow the formula perfectly.

✴ A creative mess is better than tidy idleness.

✴ Old Quilters never die, they just go to pieces.

✴ Old Quilters never die, they just fray away.

✴ As ye sew, so shall ye rip.

✴ Count your blessings. Stitch them one by one.

✴ Friends are threads of gold in the quilt of life.

✴ A day hemmed in prayer seldom unravels.

✴ A yard a day keeps the blues away.

✴ May all of your ups and downs in life be with a needle and thread.

* Blessed are the piecemakers, for they shall quilt forever!

* May your sorrows be patched and your joys quilted.

* Families are stitched together with memories.

* May your bobbin always be full!

* In the crazy quilt of life, I'm glad you're in my block of friends.

* A quilt tells a story, and the story is our past.

* If it's not about quilting, don't ask me.

* When life throws you scraps, make a quilt.

* Ask not what your fabric can do for you, but what you can do for your fabric.

* A bed without a quilt is like a sky without stars.

* Those aren't thread bits. They're debris from a creative explosion.

* I quilt; therefore, I am.

* Always trust a quilter; she knows her way around the block.

* Money can't buy happiness but it can buy a lot of fabric.

Note that the traditional role of women, based on generations and other variables, is flaunted and mocked in much of the lore. There is a defiant and honest acknowledgment that quilters are "real" and must be recognized for the true artistry and creativity involved in the design and completion of a quilt. Not only is the wit and wisdom of the quilter expressed in all these examples of lore, but also, the passion, dedication, pride, even devotion to the art of quilting. Underneath all of the lore is the undercurrent of the place of the woman in society. Quilting, and all that it represents, elevates the art form and defines it for a new ethic. An entire body of verbal folklore has developed and continues to evolve. As quilting has risen to the status of works of art, the lore will be replicated and will endure.

What are the words of the song? "I am woman, hear me roar!"

chapter 7

THE FOLK POETRY

of Quilting

THE FOLK POETRY
OF QUILTING

Whether it starts "Eenie, meenie, miney, moe" or "Icka bicka soda cracka" or "Cinderella dressed in yellow" or "When you get married," folk poetry can be identified with many different groups. They can be jump-rope rhymes, counting-out rhymes, autograph-book verses, or even taunts, but they always come anonymously from the folk and speak to some cultural concern.

Quilters are no different. Their poetry, presented anonymously or a variant of a well-known verse, is characterized by the enormous bonding quality of the quilt. Sometimes the obsession of quilting is humorously presented. But the theme is undeniable: quilting is a life force with significant meaning that cannot be ignored.

In folklore, women especially have been keepers of tradition. While they were writing in autograph books or jumping rope to cadenced rhymes, the boys were playing "Murder Ball" or some other gruesome game. Both reflected the gender, but it was the written forms of folk poetry that have stayed with us. Often they are remembered and recast in another life—one that is older and wiser. When it does reappear in the occupation or role that the folk poetry defines, the lore has a meaning different from its original purpose. Significantly, however, it is a folk formula still

being used. Perhaps it is more meaningful in the style of parody, but it is very serious in its group's definition.

Consider the popular rhyme, "Eenie, meenie, miney, moe." It has been used for decades as a counting-out rhyme to help choose sides. And the conclusion was always making someone pay for hollering! For example:

> Eenie, meenie, miney, moe
> Catch a tiger by the toe
> If he hollers, make him pay,
> Fifty dollars every day.

As with all lore, there are dozens of variants to the rhyme. And none is ever said in a vacuum; it reflects the culture in which it is spoken.

Quilters have taken this counting-out rhyme and made it their own.

> *Eenie, meenie, miney, moe*
> *Catch a quilter by the toe*
> *If she hollers, make her pay*
> *Eight fat quarters every day.*

Again, it is a parody of a well-known verse, but quilters' vocabulary is used as the punishment. Every quilter understands what is being said. Versions of this rhyme contain irony, sarcasm, inside jokes, and even jabs at the husband. Below are a few more variants. To quilters, the meaning of each is very clear and gives another stamp of approval to their "closed" folk group and love of the art.

> *Eenie, meenie, miney, moe*
> *Catch a quilter by the toe*
> *If she hollers make her pay*
> *Two hours of ripping every day.*

> *Eenie, meenie, miney, moe*
> *Catch a quilter by the toe*
> *If she hollers, make her pay*
> *Two bags of batting every day.*

> *Eenie, meenie, miney, moe*
> *Catch a quilter by the kilt*
> *If she hollers make her say*
> *You are the best quilter any day!*

> *Eenie, meenie, miney, quilt*
> *Don't let her give you guilt*
> *If she does, make her pay*
> *With Sunbonnet Sue leading the way.*

Eenie, meenie, miney, dame
Catch a quilter near her frame
If she hollers, make her pay
Watching your kids every day.

Eenie, meenie, miney, cash
See that quilter with her stash
See her eyes so shiny and clear
See her husband getting sloshed on beer.

Eenie, meenie, miney, judge
Catch a quilt with a yellow smudge
If the stain is big and messy
Use the quilt to warm ol' Bessie.

No one is certainly praising the skill in these folk poems. The importance, again, is their connection to the folk group. The humor borders on the silly, to be sure, but within that silliness is a code the quilter understands.

Weekend quilt retreats, overnights with quilts, "girls' out" quilting parties, or even some quilt guild meetings continue the tradition of the lore learned in grade school and apply it to the quilt. In a serious way, these quilting exercises are made more enjoyable with the parody humor. But make no mistake, quilting is being done and new techniques are being taught with the rhymes helping the learning process.

You will recognize the originals from the variants listed here. Some are jump-rope rhymes; some are autograph-book verses; some are joke rhymes. All are repeated traditionally within the world of the quilter.

I love coffee
I love tea
I love quilts
But they don't love me.

I love coffee
I love tea
I love quilters
Like I wish I could be.

I love coffee
I love tea
I love quilts
And they love me!

Mother sent me to the quilting store.
She said I could not stay.
I fell in love with a Lone Star Quilt.
I could not get away.

I see London
I see France,
I see Judy's
Quilted underpants.

My mother is a quilter
My father cuts the thread
And I'm a little stitchin' bitch
Cause froggin's gone to my head.
Now you are a quilter
You must be good
And make your husband
Chop all the wood.

Now you are a quilter
You must be nice
And make your kids
Beg for food only twice.

Now you are a quilter
Your time is finally here
So make your husband
Get his own damn beer.

Now you are a quilter
Piecing till early morn
So now your own husband
Can wear his socks torn.

Quilter, quilter, touch the ground
Quilter, quilter, turn around
Quilter, quilter, give a high kick
Quilter, quilter, do the splits.

Turn to the east
Turn to the west
Turn to the quilt
That you like best.

Five little quilters
Jumping on the bed
One fell off and bumped her head.
Four little quilters
Jumping on the bed
One fell off and bumped her head.
Three little quilters
Jumping on the bed
One fell off and bumped her head.

Two little quilters
Jumping on the bed
One fell off and bumped her head.
One little quilter
Jumping on the bed
One fell off and bumped her head.
No more quilters jumping on the bed
Momma called the doctor
And the doctor said
No more quilters jumping on the bed.
Save your energy and quilt instead!

Cinderella dressed in a kilt
Went upstairs to make a quilt
How many stitches did she make?
One, two, three, four, etc.

Mary had a wedding quilt
Its cloth was white as snow
And everywhere that Mary went
She brought her quilt to show.

Dolly the quilter walks like this
Dolly the quilter talks like this
Dolly the quilter smiles like this
Dolly the quilter throws a kiss.

Did you ever go a' quilting;
On a bright sunny day?
Sitting on a log
And the log rolled away.

Put your hands in your pockets
Your pockets in your pants
Did you ever see a quilter
Do the hootchy-kootchy dance?

Don't say "cheater quilt,"
Your mother will faint
Your father will fall
In a bucket of paint
Your sister will cry
Your brother will die
Your dog will call the FBI.

Monday was my washing day
Tuesday I was done
Wednesday was my ironing day
Thursday I was done
Friday was my shopping day
Saturday I was done
Sunday was my resting day
Saved for lots of fun.
Now every day's a quilting day
Housework's never done
And I don't care!!

Finally there are poems about the spouse of the quilter. This one is typical. Note the off-rhyming verse.

> *In the dark, dark world*
> *There's a dark, dark country.*
> *In the dark, dark country*
> *There's a dark, dark woods.*
> *In the dark, dark woods*
> *There's a dark, dark house.*
> *In the dark, dark house*
> *There's a man trying to quilt!*

The traditions related to quilting and the feelings engendered by a quilt are more fully realized and described in the more easily identified and longer rhyming poems. There are hundreds of poems about quilting written by poets who accurately and repeatedly speak to the romance of the quilt. Often these poems are used to accompany a popular quilt pattern to describe the emotions the quilter tried to capture. The poet's name is ascribed and the poem becomes part of a poetic tradition usually consciously done by the writer.

Other poems about quilting are transmitted orally and anonymously. These, too, in their rhythmic patterns and connotations, describe the emotions of the quilter about quilts: tradition, romance, memories, treasures, family values, history, holiday rituals, friendships, births, "sisterhood," marriages, deaths, and even spirituality, among others.

Without authorship, these poems are passed around among quilters and even used in presentations and shows. Read them aloud, as poetry should be, and you will get a deeper meaning to the lore of the quilting "folk." They describe, without comment, the "connections" quilters feel toward each other. The bond is in the symbolic quilting threads.

On Finishing an Old Quilt Top
Anonymous

Dear unknown lady of the past,
I hold your work within my hands;
A top with pattern gay and pure,
A frayed edge reveals loose strands.

The design is made of tiny scraps,
Set in a plain sugar sack ground.
Such tiny little stitches made—
A soft blue border around.

Where did you sit while piecing this?
Upon a stool by firelight bright?
Or slowly rocking on the porch
As the tired day drew into night?

What were your cares while you did work?
What plans and dreams did you spin?
I wonder why your work was stopped.
Why quilting never did begin.

My mind is filled with questions.
Were you just a girl or someone's wife?
Was yours a path of leisure?
Or a journey filled with strife?

I'll quilt this top, dear lady,
With patterns swirled and flowery,
And bond with one I'll never meet
In a sisterhood of stitchery.

In the following poem, quilting is applied to the work of God in creation and connects quilting to life. The religious connotations put quilting in a spiritual realm and underscore its significance to quilters.

I Think God Is a Quilter
Anonymous

I think God is a quilter
Who takes His needle and thread
To piece our world from nothingness
And give it form, instead.

I think God is a quilter
And everything I see
Are pieces from His careful hand
From tree to bumblebee.

I think we see God's stitches
His texture everywhere;
The velvet moss, the grainy sand,
The silky strands of hair.

I think God is a quilter;
Stitching tight and tiny rows,
Adding to my scraps and pieces,
Seaming everything He knows.

I think He cuts the patterns
From what I've thrown away.
He shows me how to use each scrap
In His redeeming way.

I think God quilts a pattern
From everything I live;
But He can only stitch the quilt
From what I choose to give.

I think God is a quilter
Stitching strength where I am weak.
Showing me that life He touches
Embraces everything I seek.

I think God is a quilter
From the patience in each thread;
Proving length of time no barrier;
Treating time a gift, instead.

I think quilts are lessons
God uses just to teach
That our pieces and our remnants
Have kaleidoscopic reach.

So, in the life I'm living
With pieces everywhere
I'll give them to the Quilter
To stitch with loving care.

I'll give them to the Quilter
Unwanted though they be
And with His work of quilting
He'll make a quilt of me.

The romance and meaning of the family bond is compared to a quilt in this poem. The connections are common in quilting circles and emphasize the values of each.

OUR FAMILY
ANONYMOUS

Our family is like a patchwork quilt
With kindness gently sewn
Each piece an original
With beauty all its own
With threads of warmth and happiness
It's lightly stitched together
To last in love throughout the years
Our family is forever.

In this poem the life of the husband of the quilter is humorously described in his own words. Nothing can stop his wife from quilting! Again, this theme of the dedicated quilter, so passionate, in fact, that her housework suffers, recurs in other folklore examples. But in a larger meaning, the message of "obsession with quilting" defines a "choice" for the woman.

ODE TO MY WIFE THE QUILTER
ANONYMOUS

She learned to quilt on Monday
Her stitches all were very fine.
She forgot to thaw out dinner
So we went out to dine.

She quilted miniatures on Tuesday
She says they are a must.
They really were quite lovely,
But she forgot to dust.

On Wednesday it was a sampler
She says stippling's fun.
What highlights! What shadows!
But the laundry wasn't done.

Her patches were on Thursday—
Green, yellow, blue, and red.
I guess she was really engrossed;
She never made the bed.

It was wall hangings on Friday.
In colors she adores.
It never bothered her at all,
The crumbs on the floors.

I found a maid on Saturday
My week is now complete.
My wife can quilt the hours away;
The house will still be neat.

Well, it's already Sunday
I think I'm about to wilt.
I cursed, I raved, I ranted.
The MAID has learned to QUILT!

Clement Moore's poem *The Night Before Christmas* may be the most popular poem ever written. Some quilter-poet used the poem's meter and rhyme to describe the hectic life of a quilter who wants to complete a project for the traditions of Christmas. Who comes to help her? Quilters! They understand the importance of the need to finish. Clear folk bonding!! This poem is one of many parodies of Moore's famous poem.

THE QUILTER'S NIGHT BEFORE CHRISTMAS
AUTHOR UNKNOWN

'Twas the night before Christmas
And the quilts were not made
The threads were all tangled,
The cookies delayed.
The stockings weren't hung, the pantry was bare,
The poor weary quilter was tearing her hair.
Stacks of fat quarters tipped over in streams.
Visions of Log Cabins had turned into dreams.
When what to her wondering eyes should appear
But a bus full of quilters with all of their gear.
They went straight to work with just a few mutters.
Sorting and stitching and brandishing cutters
The patterns emerged from all of the clutter.
Like magic the fabrics arranged in a flutter
Log Cabins, Lone Stars, Flying Geese, and Bear Tracks
Each quilt was a beauty—even the backs.
Her house how it twinkled, her quilts, how they glowed
The cookies were baking, the stockings were sewed.
Their work was all done, then they folded their frames,
And packed up their needles, without revealing their names.
They boarded the bus and checked the next address.
More quilts to be made, another quilter in distress.
She heard one voice echo as they drove out of sight,
Happy quilting to all, and to all a good night!

74

Consider the importance of quilting in the following poem. Marriage is a rite of passage and depicted in many folklore texts. There is always so much to accomplish to prepare for a "perfect" wedding day. But the day cannot be complete without the bride's quilt. Nothing, in fact, is more important, for the quilt will serve as memory for many, many years. Note, also, that the mother passed on the tradition.

THE BRIDE'S QUILT
ANONYMOUS

A maiden plans so carefully
The day when she will wed—
The cake, the gown, the flowers, and
The banquet to be fed.
There's much to be accomplished in
The days that lie ahead.
But what is most important are
The words her Mama said.
"Go fetch the cloth, the scissors, and
The needle and the thread.
We'll piece the top from calico
Of blue and green and red.
Then stretch it on the frame where back
And batting have been spread.
We'll sew until our hands have cramped.
And finger pricks have bled.
Each stitch we make within the quilt
Is Love contributed
To generations yet unborn,
'Twill be inherited.
So let our fingers fly with speed—
This project move ahead.
Your house won't be a home until
A quilt is on the bed!"

Do quilters have guilt? Some even testify to their obsessions. But the confessional will not stop them because the result of their passion will produce an heirloom.

QUILTER'S QUANDARY
ANONYMOUS

I have an affliction
Or is it an addiction?
It really is hard to say.

I wake up each morning
Sleepy and yawning,
Not ready to face the day.

All night I've thought of plans,
New patterns, designs and bands,
Until I have lost my way.

Each quilt I see
Looks good to me.
I'll make it, come what may.

The more I learn,
The more I yearn
To make a quilt that's gay.

With swatches galore
I still want more!
But somebody's got to pay!

Yes, it is an addiction,
Not an affliction,
And I know it is here to stay!

All the lore of the quilter is written in this simple poem on the "Quilting Bee." The result of all the work is not just a quilt, but as is recognized today, a "true work of art."

QUILTING BEE
ANONYMOUS

In fellowship they meet,
Their long days to invest,
Snipping and sewing, only slowing
To visit, to eat or rest.
Calico scraps, heaped on laps.
Each one an exact size and hue.
Fingers nimble with thread and thimble,
Create pretty patterns anew.
Heads bent to the task, you need not ask
If these ladies love to quilt.
Their talented touch, expresses as much
As piece onto piece it is built.
Friends try to perceive who will receive
Each quilt that is stitched from the heart,
With needlework fine, the patterns entwined
A treasure, a true work of art.

Poems about quilting, anonymously penned, are legion. The folk produce them; the folk read them; the folk pass them on. Their importance and the messages they impart cannot be overestimated: Quilting is not only my life, but it defines life itself!

chapter 8

AUNT JANE OF KENTUCKY
-- -- -- -- -- -- -- -- -- -- -- -- -- -- --
THE QUILT IN PROPER PERSPECTIVE

AUNT JANE OF KENTUCKY
THE QUILT IN PROPER PERSPECTIVE

Eliza Calvert, called Lida by everyone, was born on February 11, 1856, in Bowling Green, Kentucky. Ironically, at the time of Lida's birth, Susan B. Anthony, Elizabeth Cady Stanton, and countless other women were reforming and even rebelling against the perception of women as "feeble-brained second-class citizens." Little did they know, and history did not recall, that "baby" Lida Calvert would, through her writings, be as unassumingly determined as her famous "sisters" to elevate the cause of the American woman.

In her home state of Kentucky in the latter part of the nineteenth century, Lida wrote, spoke, and campaigned for suffrage and the Kentucky Equal Rights Association. She lectured, organized meetings, and authored prose and poetry, always working tirelessly for the rights of women.

The primary target of Lida's unabashed anger was the ruling that did not allow women control over their property or even custody of their own children. "Aunt Jane" was her answer. In the style of an interview, Lida Calvert, in 1907, published a collection of stories, *Aunt Jane of Kentucky*. Lida, the author, served as the conduit for Aunt Jane's philosophies.

Cantankerous and pulling no punches, Aunt Jane spoke for many women, not only in Kentucky, but all over America, and Lida became a best-selling author. Nothing escaped the mouth of Aunt Jane:

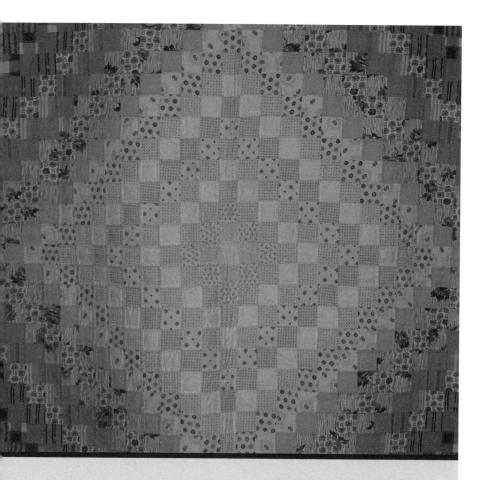

"A man's jest like a horse . . . ; you got to break him in and learn all his gaits and tricks before there's any safety or pleasure travellin' with him." (Taken from Eliza Calvert, *The Land of Long Ago* [Boston: Little Brown, 1909], p. 163.)

Or:

"I've noticed that whenever a woman's willin' to be imposed upon there's always a man standin' round ready to do the imposing." (Taken from Eliza Calvert, *Aunt Jane of Kentucky* [Boston: Little Brown, 1907], p. 27.)

But it was Aunt Jane's comments on woman's work and quilting that elevated the art to an institution. In her frank and eloquent dialogue, Lida Calvert had Aunt Jane speak for all womanhood in her famous interview.

AUNT JANE OF KENTUCKY:
THE QUILT AND THE MEANING OF LIFE

"Honey," she said, in the next breath, lowering her voice and layin' her finger on the rosebud piece, "honey, there's one thing I can't git over. Here's a piece o' Miss Penelope's dress, but where's Miss Penelope? Ain't it strange that a piece o' caliker 'll outlast you and me? Don't it look like folks ought 'o hold on to their bodies as long as other folks holds on to a piece o' the dresses they used to wear?" . . .

There lay the quilt on our knees, and the gay scraps of calico seemed to mock us with their vivid colors. Aunt Jane's cheerful voice called me back from the tombs. . . .

"Here's a piece one o' my dresses," she said; "brown ground with a red ring in it. Abram picked it out. And here's another one, that light yeller ground with the vine runnin' through it. I never had so many caliker dresses that I didn't want one more, for in my day folks used to think a caliker dress was good enough to wear anywhere. Abram knew my failin' and two or three times a year he'd bring me a dress when he come from town. And the dresses he'd pick out always suited me better'n than ones I picked.

"I ricollect I finished this quilt the summer before Mary Frances was born and Sally Ann and Milly Amos and Maria Petty come over and give me a lift on the quiltin'. Here's Milly's work, here's Sally Ann's and here's Maria's."

I looked, but my inexperienced eye could see no difference in the handiwork of the three women. Aunt Jane saw my look of incredulity.

"Now, child," she said, earnestly, "you think I'm foolin' you, but there jest as much difference in folks' sewin' as there is in their handwritin'.

Milly made a fine stitch, but she couldn't keep on the line to save her life. Maria never could make a reg'lar stitch, some'd be long and some short, and Sally Ann's was reg'lar, but all of 'em coarse. I can see 'em now stoopin' over the quiltin' frames—Milly talkin' as hard as she sewed, Sally Ann throwin' in a word now and then, and Maria never openin' her mouth except to ask for the thread or the chalk. I ricollect they come over after dinner and we got the quilt out o' the frames long before sundown, and the next day I begun bindin' it and I got the premium on it that year at the Fair.

"I hardly ever showed a quilt at the Fair that I didn't take the premium, but here's one quilt that Sarah Jane Mitchell beat me on. . . .

It makes me laugh jest to think o' that time and how happy Sarah Jane was. It was way back yonder in the fifties (*1850s*). I ricollect we had a mighty fine Fair that year. The crops was all fine that season, and such apples and pears and grapes you never did see. The Floral Hall was full o' things, and the whole county turned out to go to the Fair. Abram and me got there the first day bright and early, and we was walkin' around the amp'itheater and lookin' at the townfolks and the sights, and we met Sally Ann. She stopped us, and says she, 'Sarah Jane Mitchell's got a quilt in the Floral Hall in competition with yours and Milly Amos'. Says I, 'Is that all the competition there is?' And Sally Ann says, 'All that amounts to anything. There's one more, but it's about as bad a piece o' sewin' as Sarah Jane's, and that looks like it'd hardly hold together till the Fair's over. And,' says she, 'I don't believe there'll be any more. It looks like this was an off year on that particular kind o' quilt. I didn't get mine done,' says she, 'and neither did Maria Petty, and maybe it's a good thing after all.'

"Well, I saw in a minute what Sally Ann was aimin' at. And I says to Abram, 'Abram, haven't you got somethin' to do with the app'intin' the judges for the women's things?' And he says, 'Yes.' And I says, 'Well, you see to it that Sally Ann gits app'inted to help judge the caliker quilts.' And bless your soul Abram got me and Sally Ann both app'inted. The other judge was Mis' Doctor Brigham, o' the town ladies. We told her all about what we wanted to do and she jest laughed and says, 'Well, if that ain't the kindest, nicest thin! Of course we'll do it.'

"Seein' that I had a quilt there, I hadn't a bit o' business bein' a judge; but the first thing I did was to fold my quilt up and hide it under Maria Petty's big worsted quilt, and then we pinned the blue ribbon on Sarah Jane's and the red on Milly's. I'd fixed it all up with Milly and she was jest as willin' as I was for Sarah Jane to have the premium. There was jest one thing I was afraid of: Milly was a good-hearted woman, but she never had much control over her tongue. And I says to her, says I: 'Milly, it's mighty good of you to give up your chance for the premium, but if Sarah Jane ever finds it out, that'll spoil everything. For,' says I, 'there ain't any kindness in doin' a person a favor and then tellin' everybody about it.' And Milly laughed and says she: 'I know what you mean, Aunt Jane. It's mighty hard for me to keep from tellin' everything I know and some things I don't know, but', says she, 'I'm never goin' to tell this, even to Sam.' And she kept her word, too. Every once in a while she'd come up to me and whisper, 'I ain't told it yet, Aunt Jane, jest to see me laugh.'

"As soon as the doors was open, after we'd all got through judgin' and puttin' on the ribbons, Milly went and hunted Sarah Jane up and told her that her quilt had the blue ribbon. They said the pore thing like to 'a' fainted for joy. She turned right white and had to lean up against the post for a while before she could git to the Floral Hall. I never shall forget her face. It was worth a dozen premiums to me, and Milly, too. She jest stood lookin' at that quilt and the blue ribbon on it and her eyes was full o' tears and her lips quiverin', and then she started off and brought the children to look at 'Mammy's quilt. She met Sam on the way out and says she: 'Sam what do you reckon? My quilt took the premium.' And I believe in my soul Sam was as much pleased as Sarah Jane. He came saunterin' up, tryin' to look unconcerned, but anybody could see he was mighty well satisfied. It does a husband and wife a heap o' good to be proud of each other, and I reckin' that was the first time Sam ever had cause to be proud o' pore Sarah Jane. It's my belief that he thought more o' Sarah Jane all the rest o' her life jest on account o' that premium. Me and Sally Ann helped her pick it out. She had her choice betwixt a butter-dish and a cup, and she took the cup. Folks used to laugh and say that that cup was the only thing in Sarah Jane's house that was kept clean and bright and if it hadn't a' been solid silver she'd a' wore it all out rubbin' it up. Sarah Jane died o' pneumonia about three or four years after that, and the folks that nursed her said she wouldn't take a drink o' water or a dose o' medicine out o' any cup but that. There's some folks, child, that don't have to do anything but walk along and hold out their hands, and the premiums jest naturally fall into 'em; and there's others that work and strive the best they know how, and nothin' ever seems to come to 'em; and I reckon nobody but the Lord and Sarah Jane knows how much happiness she got out o' that cup. I'm thankful she had that much pleasure before she died."

Aunt Jane was regarding (her "special") a quilt with worshipful eyes. (She had made it from a pattern her granddaughter copied from a church floor in Florence, Italy.)

"Many a time while I was piecin' that," she said, "I thought about the man that laid the pavement in that old church, and wondered what his name was, and how he looked, and what he'd think if he knew there was a old woman down here in Kentucky usin' his patterns to make a bedquilt." . . .

"Did you ever think, child," she said, presently, "how much piecin' a quilt's like livin' a life? And as for sermons, why, they ain't no better sermon to me than a patchwork quilt, and the doctrines is right there a heap plainer'n they are in the catechism. Many a time I've set and listened to Parson Page preachin' about predestination and free-will and I've said to myself, 'Well, I ain't never been through Centre College up at Danville, but if I could jest get up in the pulpit with one of my quilts, I could make it a heap plainer to folks than parson's makin' it with all his big words.' You see, you start out with jest so much caliker; you don't go to the store and pick it out and buy it, but the neighbors will give you a piece here and a piece there, and you'll have a piece left every time you cut out a dress, and you take jest what happens to come. And that's like predestination. But when it come to the cuttin' out, why you're free to choose your own pattern. You can give the same kind o' pieces to two persons, and one'll make a nine-patch and one'll make a wild goose chase, and there's be two quilts made out o' the same kind of pieces and jest as different as they can be. And that is jest the way with livin'. The Lord sends us the pieces, but we can cut 'em out and put 'em together pretty much to suit ourselves, and there's a heap more in the cuttin' out and the sewin' than there is in the caliker.

"And when it comes to puttin' the pieces together, there's another time when we're free. You don't trust to luck for the caliker to put your quilt together with; you go to the store and pick it out for yourself, any color you like. There's folks that always looks on the bright side and makes the best of everything, and that's like puttin' your quilt together with blue or pink or white or some other pretty color and there's folks that never see anything but the dark side and always lookin' for trouble, and treasurin' it up after they git it and there puttin' their lives together with black, jest like you would put a quilt together with some dark, ugly color. You can spoil the prettiest quilt pieces that ever was made jest by puttin' 'em together with the wrong color, and the best sort o' life is miserable if you don't look at things right and think about 'em right.

"Then there's another thing. I've seen folks piece and piece, but when it come to puttin' the blocks together and quiltin' and linin' it, they'd give out; and that's like folks that do a little here and a little there, but their lives ain't of much use after all, any more'n a lot o' loose pieces o' patchwork. And then while you're livin' your life, it looks pretty much like a jumble o' quilt pieces before they're put together, but when you git through with it, or pretty right through, as I am now, you'll see the use and the purpose of everything in it. Everything'll be in its right place jest like the squares in this four-patch; and one piece may be pretty and another one ugly, but at all looks right when you see it finished and joined together.

"I've been a hard worker all my life," she said, seating herself and folding her hands restfully, "but 'most all my work has been the kind that 'perishes with the usin',' as the Bible says. That's the discouragin' thing about a woman's work. Milly Amos used to say that if a woman was to see all the dishes that she had to wash before she died, piled up right before her in one pile, she'd lie down and die right then and there. I've always had the name of bein' a good housekeeper, but when I'm dead and gone there ain't anybody goin' to think o' the floor I've swept, and the tables I've scrubbed, and the old clothes I've patched, and the stockin's I've darned. Abram might 'a' remembered it, but he ain't here. But when one o' my grandchildren or great-grandchildren see one o' these quilts, they'll think of Aunt Jane and, wherever I am then, I'll know I ain't forgotten." . . .

"Now some folks have money to build monuments with great, tall, marble pillars, with angels on top of 'em, like you see in Cave Hill and them big city buryin' grounds. And some folks can build churches and schools an' hospitals to keep folks in mind of 'em, but all the work I've got to leave behind me is jest these quilts, and sometimes, when I'm settin' here, workin' with my caliker and gingham pieces, I'll finish off a block and I laugh and say to myself, 'Well, here's another stone for the monument.'

"I reckon you think, child, that a caliker or a worsted quilt is a curious sort of a monument, 'bout as perishable as the sweepin' and scrubbin' and mendin'. But if folks values things rightly, and knows how to take care of 'em, there ain't many things that'll last longer'n a quilt."

(Taken from Calvert, Aunt Jane of Kentucky, pp. 63–79.)

The essence of the art of quilting and how the "folk" are defined comes through in this conversation with Aunt Jane. Note how the women gathered around the quilt frame, compared the quality of quilt stitches, competed for the "premium," and the pattern making and the religious references. All of these are part of the lore of the quilter. More importantly, note the reverence, pride, passion, and even a kind of spiritual reckoning that quilting can produce. There is, again, "control of my world" and "I choose the patterns and the colors" and "my work, with humble beginnings, will become a monument."

As stated many times, quilters are a special folk group. They maintain their lore but they successfully have reached beyond the quilt frame and the tangible connection with their "own" to create functional and beautiful works of art.

Yes, quilters know what they are "doing in the ditch!" They are documenting history and memories and treasures for generations to come. Carpe Quiltem!!

THE QUILT REPRODUCES!

AFTERWORD !
THE QUILT REPRODUCES

Quietly, steadily, conscientiously, the American woman has been quilting for hundreds of years. Preserving material, recording history through fabric, remembering family or friends with colorful scraps, and, without fanfare, creating a work of original art—the woman was the first conservator, the uneducated but accurate historian, the keeper of tradition, and the definer of the American Character.

The quilters of the nineteenth and early twentieth centuries would marvel at the exponential popularity and artistry of the current art of quilting. They would not be upset, as some suggest, at the modern methods now used, because they would recognize the same passion in today's quilters as they had: to create a memory and a lore for generations.

In the purest sense of the definition of folklore, quilting is now expressed in myriad ways: dolls, clothing, purses, jewelry, wall hangings, miniature quilts, pillows, hats, pin cushions, and even underwear. Importantly, also, the American male has become a force in the quilt world. Many men make quilts with traditional patterns or design original award-winning quilts, and some even quit their own careers to support their wives' quilting. (The irony

is certainly not lost here: "Men," who kept women "in their place" for decades and defined them as not capable of leaving the home, have now come "over to the other side," as some female quilters say. But there is no bitterness. There is only, and importantly, a larger folk group evolving with the same mission.)

Several national quilt shows are planned yearly with hundreds of quilts displayed and thousands of dollars given in prizes. Several national quilt museums have been built to house the artistry and history that is the American quilt. Several archives have been established to further the research on the history of the American quilt. Not several, but hundreds of quilt guilds and clubs have been established that echo the quilting bee in an explosive style. Quilt stores devoted to the sale of all-things-quilts have become "religious destinations" all over America. Novelists and historians have documented the charm and the meaning of the quilt as both symbol and fact. And there are dramas about quilts where the quilt becomes a character used to advance the story. There are symposia on quilts; debates on the "meaning" of the quilt; workshops for beginners to experts; even quilting retreats of a weekend or several days are common as expanded quilting bees. Perhaps, most significantly, the American quilt has become a phenomenon throughout the world and has motivated craftspeople, often in some remote village or hamlet, to take up the art.

Research Methodology

Too often the term "folklore" is connected incorrectly with trivia, old wives' tales, "made-up" facts, and even fibs. To paraphrase comedian Rodney Dangerfield, "Folklore gets no respect!" This lack of recognition is, thankfully, with the general population, because the study of folklore, even the science of folklore, has been a part of academia for hundreds of years. Major universities around the world offer graduate programs, including a PhD, for serious studies about the oral traditions that are folklore and their context in the fabric of a culture.

There are compendia, collections, indices, and archives in major libraries all over the world that document and annotate folklore texts and their applications over centuries. The trained folklorist must have intimate knowledge of these resources to help this "digging" for meaning. It is the trained and certified methodology of fieldwork, with its detailed progressive steps, which is conscientiously and consistently applied for the research of all lore. Depending on the genre of the folklore, the work in the field is tailored to collect all the necessary background.

For my fieldwork in the lore of the quilt, my investigative techniques as part of the process were primarily the interview, participative management, and the questionnaire. As I explained earlier, travelling to quilt shows, judging quilt shows, and meeting quilters at all levels, I was both able to interview them and observe their work habits and craftsmanship. I was always aware of the materials used, the equipment used, the process followed, and the context in which the craftsman carried out the task.

I also used a consistent set of interview questions/questionnaires to ensure clarity with my results. Below is an example of some of the questions I used when talking to hundreds of quilters:

What are the traditional names for quilt patterns you can remember from you quilting days? Have you made any of them? Where do you think the names of the quilts came from? Do you ever name a quilt?

What materials are your favorites to use in your quilting? Where did/do you get the fabrics? What types of needles do you use or have used? What types of frames do you use or have used?

What patterns do you usually follow in the quilting process itself? Where did you get them? Some quilters are famous for their stitches. In your mind, what makes a good stitched quilt?

Did you or do you ever participate in a quilting party or quilt guild or church quilting club? Where were they held? Who attended? Was their purpose about quilting only? Any refreshments? What time of the day were they held on which day of the week?

Do you know of any customs associated with quilts or quilting?

What does a "show" quilt mean to you? What does a "bridal quilt" mean? Do you have any names for other "special quilts?"

What do you do with used or worn quilts?

Do you remember any proverbs, sayings, humor, songs, rhymes, or superstitions which refer to quilts in any way?

What is most appealing to you about quilting?

How did you learn to quilt? Have you taught anyone to quilt?

What are your thoughts on machine quilting as compared to hand
    quilting?

Are most of yout quilts patchwork or appliqué? Why?

The women (mostly) and men quilters I have talked with over the
years have been very generous in their conversation about the art of
quilting. They understood the need to record the techniques of their
craft so that the tradition would never be lost. This work is their book.

About the Author

Dr. John L. Oldani (a.k.a. Dr. Jack to his students) has collected and documented American folklore for years. He established an archive for research with a strong emphasis on the American quilt and the lore surrounding its history. Dr. Oldani has produced quilt shows, served as a judge at national shows, and has written and spoken on the meaning of the American quilt as seen through folklore.

As a professor for more than thirty years, Dr. Oldani has been inducted into the Professor Hall of Fame. He was the writer for the "Johnny Cash American Folklore" radio program and was guest/host on national radio outlets on American Folklore for twenty-five years. He is the author of *Sweetness Preserved: The Story of the Crown Candy Kitchen* and *Passing It On: Folklore of St. Louis*.